AF306761

Defoe Abbott Marx Hardy Melville Montaigne Machiavelli Haggard Chesterton Cooper Emerson Joyce Austen Hugo Eliot Grimm

Stoker Carroll Christie Maupassant Byron Molière Schiller

Wilde Garnett Einstein Fitzgerald Engels Hawthorne Smith Kafka Hall

Goethe Dostoyevsky Willis

Cotton Kipling Doyle

Baum Henry Nietzsche Balzac

Leslie Dumas Flaubert Turgenev Crane

Stockton Vatsyayana Verne

Burroughs Vinci

Curtis Tocqueville Gogol Busch

Homer Widger Tolstoy Whitman

Darwin Thoreau Twain Scott Plato Harte

Potter Zola Lawrence Dickens

Kant Freud Jowett Stevenson Burton Hesse

Andersen Cooke

London Descartes Cervantes Voltaire

Poe Aristotle Wells

Hale James Hastings Cooke

Bunner Shakespeare Irving

Richter Chambers

Doré Dante Chekhov da Shaw Benedict Alcott

Swift Wodehouse Pushkin

Newton

tredition

tredition was established in 2006 by Sandra Latusseck and Soenke Schulz. Based in Hamburg, Germany, tredition offers publishing solutions to authors and publishing houses, combined with worldwide distribution of printed and digital book content. tredition is uniquely positioned to enable authors and publishing houses to create books on their own terms and without conventional manufacturing risks.

For more information please visit: www.tredition.com

TREDITION CLASSICS

This book is part of the TREDITION CLASSICS series. The creators of this series are united by passion for literature and driven by the intention of making all public domain books available in printed format again - worldwide. Most TREDITION CLASSICS titles have been out of print and off the bookstore shelves for decades. At tredition we believe that a great book never goes out of style and that its value is eternal. Several mostly non-profit literature projects provide content to tredition. To support their good work, tredition donates a portion of the proceeds from each sold copy. As a reader of a TREDITION CLASSICS book, you support our mission to save many of the amazing works of world literature from oblivion. See all available books at www.tredition.com.

Project Gutenberg

The content for this book has been graciously provided by Project Gutenberg. Project Gutenberg is a non-profit organization founded by Michael Hart in 1971 at the University of Illinois. The mission of Project Gutenberg is simple: To encourage the creation and distribution of eBooks. Project Gutenberg is the first and largest collection of public domain eBooks.

History of the Revolt of the Netherlands —Volume 03

Friedrich Schiller

Imprint

This book is part of TREDITION CLASSICS

Author: Friedrich Schiller
Cover design: Buchgut, Berlin – Germany

Publisher: tredition GmbH, Hamburg - Germany
ISBN: 978-3-8424-6446-9

www.tredition.com
www.tredition.de

BOOK III.

CONSPIRACY OF THE NOBLES

1565. Up to this point the general peace had it appears been the sincere wish of the Prince of Orange, the Counts Egmont and Horn, and their friends. They had pursued the true interests of their sovereign as much as the general weal; at least their exertions and their actions had been as little at variance with the former as with the latter. Nothing bad as yet occurred to make their motives suspected, or to manifest in them a rebellious spirit. What they had done they had done in discharge of their bounden duty as members of a free state, as the representatives of the nation, as advisers of the king, as men of integrity and honor. The only weapons they had used to oppose the encroachments of the court had been remonstrances, modest complaints, petitions. They had never allowed themselves to be so far carried away by a just zeal for their good cause as to transgress the limits of prudence and moderation which on many occasions are so easily overstepped by party spirit. But all the nobles of the republic did not now listen to the voice of that prudence; all did not abide within the bounds of moderation.

While in the council of state the great question was discussed whether the nation was to be miserable or not, while its sworn deputies summoned to their assistance all the arguments of reason and of equity, and while the middle-classes and the people contented themselves with empty complaints, menaces, and curses, that part of the nation which of all seemed least called upon, and on whose support least reliance had been placed, began to take more active measures. We have already described a class of the nobility whose services and wants Philip at his accession had not considered it necessary to remember. Of these by far the greater number had asked for promotion from a much more urgent reason than a love of the mere honor. Many of them were deeply sunk in debt, from which by their own resources they could not hope to emancipate themselves. When then, in filling up appointments, Philip passed them over he wounded them in a point far more sensitive than their pride. In these suitors he had by his neglect raised up so many idle spies and merciless judges of his actions, so many collectors and propagators of malicious rumor. As their pride did not quit them with their prosperity, so now, driven by necessity, they trafficked with the sole capital which they could not alienate — their nobility and the political influence of their names; and brought into circulation a coin which only in such a period could have found currency — their protection. With a self-pride to which they gave the more scope as it was all they could now call their own, they looked upon themselves as a strong intermediate power between the sovereign and the citizen, and believed themselves called upon to hasten to the rescue of the oppressed state, which looked imploringly to them for succor. This idea was ludicrous only so far as their self-conceit was concerned in it; the advantages which they contrived to draw from it were substantial enough. The Protestant merchants, who held in their hands the chief part of the wealth of the Netherlands, and who believed they could not at any price purchase too dearly the undisturbed exercise of their religion, did not fail to make use of this class of people who stood idle in the market and ready to be hired. These very men whom at any other time the merchants, in the pride of riches, would most probably have looked down upon, now appeared likely to do them good service through their numbers, their courage, their credit with the populace, their enmity to the government, nay, through their beggarly pride itself and their despair. On these grounds they zealously endeavored to form a close union with them, and diligently fostered the disposition for rebellion, while they also used every means to keep alive their high opinions of themselves, and, what was most important, lured their poverty by well-applied pecuniary assistance and glittering promises. Few of them were so utterly insignificant as not to possess some influence, if not personally, yet at least by their relationship with higher and more powerful nobles; and if united they would be able to raise a formidable voice against the crown. Many of them had either already joined the new sect or were secretly inclined to it; and even those who were zealous Roman Catholics had political or private grounds enough to set them against the decrees of Trent and

the Inquisition. All, in fine, felt the call of vanity sufficiently powerful not to allow the only moment to escape them in which they
might possibly make some figure in the republic.

But much as might be expected from the co-operation of these
men in a body it would have been futile and ridiculous to build any
hopes on any one of them singly; and the great difficulty was to
effect a union among them. Even to bring them together some unu-
sual occurrence was necessary, and fortunately such an incident
presented itself. The nuptials of Baron Montigny, one of the Belgian
nobles, as also those of the Prince Alexander of Parma, which took
place about this time in Brussels, assembled in that town a great
number of the Belgian nobles. On this occasion relations met relations; new friendships were formed and old renewed; and while the
distress of the country was the topic of conversation wine and mirth
unlocked lips and hearts, hints were dropped of union among
themselves, and of an alliance with foreign powers. These acci-
dental meetings soon led to concealed ones, and public discussions
gave rise to secret consultations. Two German barons, moreover, a
Count of Holle and a Count of Schwarzenberg, who at this time
were on a visit to the Netherlands, omitted nothing to awaken expectations of assistance from their neighbors. Count Louis of Nassau, too, had also a short time before visited several German courts
to ascertain their sentiments.

> [It was not without cause that the Prince of Or-
> ange suddenly disappeared from Brussels in order
> to be present at the election of a king of Rome in
> Frankfort. An assembly of so many German princ-
> es must have greatly favored a negotiation.]

It has even been asserted that secret emissaries of the Admiral Co-
ligny were seen at this time in Brabant, but this, however, may be
reasonably doubted.

If ever a political crisis was favorable to an attempt at revolution
it was the present. A woman at the helm of government; the governors of provinces disaffected themselves and disposed to wink at
insubordination in others; most of the state counsellors quite ineffi-
cient; no army to fall back upon; the few troops there were long
since discontented on account of the outstanding arrears of pay, and

already too often deceived by false promises to be enticed by new; commanded, moreover, by officers who despised the Inquisition from their hearts, and would have blushed to draw a sword in its behalf; and, lastly, no money in the treasury to enlist new troops or to hire foreigners. The court at Brussels, as well as the three councils, not only divided by internal dissensions, but in the highest degree — venal and corrupt; the regent without full powers to act on the spot, and the king at a distance; his adherents in the provinces few, uncertain, and dispirited; the faction numerous and powerful; two-thirds of the people irritated against popery and desirous of a change — such was the unfortunate weakness of the government, and the more unfortunate still that this weakness was so well known to its enemies!

In order to unite so many minds in the prosecution of a common object a leader was still wanting, and a few influential names to give political weight to their enterprise. The two were supplied by Count Louis of Nassau and Henry Count Brederode, both members of the most illustrious houses of the Belgian nobility, who voluntarily placed themselves at the head of the undertaking. Louis of Nassau, brother of the Prince of Orange, united many splendid qualities which made him worthy of appearing on so noble and important a stage. In Geneva, where he studied, he had imbibed at once a hatred to the hierarchy and a love to the new religion, and on his return to his native country had not failed to enlist proselytes to his opinions. The republican bias which his mind had received in that school kindled in him a bitter hatred of the Spanish name, which animated his whole conduct and only left him with his latest breath. Popery and Spanish rule were in his mind identical — as indeed they were in reality — and the abhorrence which he entertained for the one helped to strengthen his dislike for the other. Closely as the brothers agreed in their inclinations and aversions the ways by which each sought to gratify them were widely dissimilar. Youth and an ardent temperament did not allow the younger brother to follow the tortuous course through which the elder wound himself to his object. A cold, calm circumspection carried the latter slowly but surely to his aim, and with a pliable subtilty he made all things subserve his purpose; with a foolhardy impetuosity which overthrew all obstacles, the other at times compelled success, but oftener accelerated disaster. For this reason William was a general and Louis never more than an adventurer; a sure and powerful arm if only it were directed by a wise head. Louis' pledge once given was good forever; his alliances survived every vicissitude, for they were mostly formed in the pressing moment of necessity, and misfortune binds more firmly than thoughtless joy. He loved his brother as dearly as he did his cause, and for the latter he died.

Henry of Brederode, Baron of Viane and Burgrave of Utrecht, was descended from the old Dutch counts who formerly ruled that province as sovereign princes. So ancient a title endeared him to the people, among whom the memory of their former lords still survived, and was the more treasured the less they felt they had gained by the change. This hereditary splendor increased the self-conceit of a man upon whose tongue the glory of his ancestors continually hung, and who dwelt the more on former greatness, even amidst its ruins, the more unpromising the aspect of his own condition became. Excluded from the honors and employments to which, in his opinion, his own merits and his noble ancestry fully entitled him (a squadron of light cavalry being all which was entrusted to him), he hated the government, and did not scruple boldly to canvass and to rail at its measures. By these means he won the hearts of the people. He also favored in secret the evangelical belief; less, however, as a conviction of his better reason than as an opposition to the government. With more loquacity than eloquence, and more audacity than courage, he was brave rather from not believing in danger than from being superior to it. Louis of Nassau burned for the cause which he defended, Brederode for the glory of being its defender; the former was satisfied in acting for his party, the latter discontented if he did not stand at its head. No one was more fit to lead off the dance in a rebellion, but it could hardly have a worse ballet-master. Contemptible as his threatened designs really were, the illusion of the multitude might have imparted to them weight and terror if it had occurred to them to set up a pretender in his person. His claim to the possessions of his ancestors was an empty name; but even a name was now sufficient for the general disaffection to rally round. A pamphlet which was at the time disseminated amongst the people openly called him the heir of Holland; and his engraved portrait, which was publicly exhibited, bore the boastful inscription: —

Sum Brederodus ego, Batavae non infima gentis
Gloria, virtutem non unica pagina claudit.

(1565.) Besides these two, there were others also from among the most illustrious of the Flemish nobles the young Count Charles of Mansfeld, a son of that nobleman whom we have found among the most zealous royalists; the Count Kinlemburg; two Counts of Bergen and of Battenburg; John of Marnix, Baron of Toulouse; Philip of Marnix, Baron of St. Aldegonde; with several others who joined the league, which, about the middle of November, in the year 1565, was formed at the house of Von Hammes, king at arms of the Golden Fleece. Here it was that six men decided the destiny of their country as formerly a few confederates consummated the liberty of Switzerland, kindled the torch of a forty years' war, and laid the basis of a freedom which they themselves were never to enjoy. The objects of the league were set forth in the following declaration, to which Philip of Marnix was the first to subscribe his name: "Whereas certain ill-disposed persons, under the mask of a pious zeal, but in reality under the impulse of avarice and ambition, have by their evil counsels persuaded our most gracious sovereign the king to introduce into these countries the abominable tribunal of the Inquisition, a tribunal diametrically opposed to all laws, human and divine, and in cruelty far surpassing the barbarous institutions of heathenism; which raises the inquisitors above every other power, and debases man to a perpetual bondage, and by its snares exposes the honest citizen to a constant fear of death, inasmuch as any one (priest, it may be, or a faithless friend, a Spaniard or a reprobate), has it in his power at any moment to cause whom he will to be dragged before that tribunal, to be placed in confinement, condemned, and executed without the accused ever being allowed to face his accuser, or to adduce proof of his innocence; we, therefore, the undersigned, have bound ourselves to watch over the safety of our families, our estates, and our own persons. To this we hereby pledge ourselves, and to this end bind ourselves as a sacred fraternity, and vow with a solemn oath to oppose to the best of our power the introduction of this tribunal into these countries, whether it be attempted openly or secretly, and under whatever name it may be disguised. We at the same time declare that we are far from intending anything unlawful against the king our sovereign; rather is it our unalterable purpose to support and defend the royal prerogative, and to maintain peace, and, as far as lies in our power, to put down all rebellion. In accordance with this purpose we have sworn, and now again swear, to hold sacred the government, and to respect it both in word and deed, which witness Almighty God!

"Further, we vow and swear to protect and defend one another, in all times and places, against all attacks whatsoever touching the articles which are set forth in this covenant. We hereby bind ourselves that no accusation of any of our followers, in whatever name it may be clothed, whether rebellion, sedition, or otherwise, shall avail to annul our oath towards the accused, or absolve us from our obligation towards him. No act which is directed against the Inquisition can deserve the name of a rebellion. Whoever, therefore, shall be placed in arrest on any such charge, we here pledge ourselves to assist him to the utmost of our ability, and to endeavor by every allowable means to effect his liberation. In this, however, as in all matters, but especially in the conduct of all measures against the tribunal of the Inquisition, we submit ourselves to the general regulations of the league, or to the decision of those whom we may unanimously appoint our counsellors and leaders.

"In witness hereof, and in confirmation of this our common league and covenant, we call upon the holy name of the living God, maker of heaven and earth, and of all that are therein, who searches the hearts, the consciences, and the thoughts, and knows the purity of ours. We implore the aid of the Holy Spirit, that success and honor may crown our undertaking, to the glory of His name, and to the peace and blessing of our country!"

This covenant was immediately translated into several languages, and quickly disseminated through the provinces. To swell the league as speedily as possible each of the confederates assembled all his friends, relations, adherents, and retainers. Great banquets were held, which lasted whole days—irresistible temptations for a sensual, luxurious people, in whom the deepest wretchedness could not stifle the propensity for voluptuous living. Whoever repaired to these banquets—and every one was welcome—was plied with officious assurances of friendship, and, when heated with wine, carried away by the example of numbers, and overcome by the fire of a wild eloquence. The hands of many were guided while they subscribed their signatures; the hesitating were derided, the pusillanimous threatened, the scruples of loyalty clamored down; some even were quite ignorant what they were signing, and were ashamed afterwards to inquire. To many whom mere levity brought to the entertainment the general enthusiasm left no choice, while the splendor of the confederacy allured the mean, and its numbers encouraged the timorous. The abettors of the league had not scrupled at the artifice of counterfeiting the signature and seals of the Prince of Orange, Counts Egmont, Horn, Mcgen, and others, a trick which won them hundreds of adherents. This was done especially with a view of influencing the officers of the army, in order to be safe in this quarter, if matters should come at last to violence. The device succeeded with many, especially with subalterns, and Count Brederode even drew his sword upon an ensign who wished time for consideration. Men of all classes and conditions signed it. Religion made no difference. Roman Catholic priests even were associates of the league. The motives were not the same with all, but the pretext was similar. The Roman Catholics desired simply the abolition of the Inquisition, and a mitigation of the edicts; the Protestants aimed at unlimited freedom of conscience. A few daring spirits only entertained so bold a project as the overthrow of the present government, while the needy and indigent based the vilest hopes on a general anarchy. A farewell entertainment, which about this time was given to the Counts Schwarzenberg and Holle in Breda, and another shortly afterwards in Hogstraten, drew many of the principal nobility to these two places, and of these several had already signed the covenant. The Prince of Orange, Counts Egmont, Horn, and Megen were present at the latter banquet, but without any concert or design, and without having themselves any share in the league, although one of Egmont's own secretaries and some of the servants of the other three noblemen had openly joined it. At this entertainment three hundred persons gave in their adhesion to the covenant, and the question was mooted whether the whole body should present themselves before the regent armed or unarmed, with a declaration or with a petition? Horn and Orange (Egmont would not countenance the business in any way) were called in as arbiters upon this point, and they decided in favor of the more moderate and submissive procedure. By taking this office upon them they exposed themselves to the charge of having in no very covert manner lent their sanction to the enterprise of the confederates. In compliance, therefore, with their advice, it was determined to present their address unarmed, and in the form of a petition, and a day was appointed on which they should assemble in Brussels.

The first intimation the regent received of this conspiracy of the nobles was given by the Count of Megen soon after his return to the capital. "There was," he said, "an enterprise on foot; no less than three hundred of the nobles were implicated in it; it referred to religion; the members of it had bound themselves together by an oath; they reckoned much on foreign aid; she would soon know more about it." Though urgently pressed, he would give her no further information. "A nobleman," he said, "had confided it to him under the seal of secrecy, and he had pledged his word of honor to him." What really withheld him from giving her any further explanation was, in all probability, not so much any delicacy about his honor, as his hatred of the Inquisition, which he would not willingly do anything to advance. Soon after him, Count Egmont delivered to the regent a copy of the covenant, and also gave her the names of the conspirators, with some few exceptions. Nearly about the same time the Prince of Orange wrote to her: "There was, as he had heard, an army enlisted, four hundred officers were already named, and twenty thousand men would presently appear in arms." Thus the rumor was intentionally exaggerated, and the danger was multiplied in every mouth.

The regent, petrified with alarm at the first announcement of these tidings, and guided solely by her fears, hastily called together all the members of the council of state who happened to be then in Brussels, and at the same time sent a pressing summons to the Prince of Orange and Count Horn, inviting them to resume their seats in the senate. Before the latter could arrive she consulted with Egmont, Megen, and Barlaimont what course was to be adopted in the present dangerous posture of affairs. The question debated was whether it would be better to have recourse to arms or to yield to the emergency and grant the demands of the confederates; or whether they should be put off with promises, and an appearance of compliance, in order to gain time for procuring instructions from Spain, and obtaining money and troops? For the first plan the requisite supplies were wanting, and, what was equally requisite, confidence in the army, of which there seemed reason to doubt whether it had not been already gained by the conspirators. The second expedient would it was quite clear never be sanctioned by the king; besides it would serve rather to raise than depress the courage of the confederates; while, on the other hand, a compliance with their reasonable demands and a ready unconditional pardon of the past would in all probability stifle the rebellion in the cradle. The last opinion was supported by Megen and Egmont but opposed by Barlaimont. "Rumor," said the latter, "had exaggerated the matter; it is impossible that so formidable an armament could have been prepared so secretly and, so rapidly. It was but a band of a few outcasts and desperadoes, instigated by two or three enthusiasts, nothing more. All will be quiet after a few heads have been struck off." The regent determined to await the opinion of the council of state, which was shortly to assemble; in the meanwhile, however, she was not inactive. The fortifications in the most important places were inspected and the necessary repairs speedily executed; her ambassadors at foreign courts received orders to redouble their vigilance; expresses were sent off to Spain. At the same time she caused the report to be revived of the near advent of the king, and in her external deportment put on a show of that imperturbable firmness which awaits attack without intending easily to yield to it. At the end of March (four whole months consequently from the framing of the covenant), the whole state council assembled in Brussels. There were present the Prince of Orange, the Duke of Arschot, Counts Egmont, Bergen, Megen, Aremberg, Horn, Hosstraten, Barlaimont, and others; the Barons Montigny and Hachicourt, all the knights of the Golden Fleece, with the President Viglius, State Counsellor Bruxelles, and the other assessors of the privy council. Several letters were produced which gave a clearer insight into the nature and objects of the conspiracy. The extremity to which the regent was reduced gave the disaffected a power which on the present occasion they did not neglect to use. Venting their long suppressed indignation, they indulged in bitter complaints against the court and against the government. "But lately," said the Prince of Orange, "the king sent forty thousand gold florins to the Queen of Scotland to support her in her undertakings against England, and he allows his Netherlands to be burdened with debt. Not to mention the unseasonableness of this subsidy and its fruitless expenditure, why should he bring upon us the resentment of a queen, who is both so important to us as a friend and as an enemy so much to be dreaded?" The prince did not even refrain on the present occasion from glancing at the concealed hatred which the king was suspected of cherishing against the family of Nassau and against him in particular. "It is well known," he said, "that he has plotted with the hereditary enemies of my house to take away my life, and that he waits with impatience only for a suitable opportunity." His example opened the lips of Count Horn also, and of many others besides, who with passionate vehemence descanted on their own merits and the ingratitude of the king. With difficulty did the regent succeed in silencing the tumult and in recalling attention to the proper subject of the debate. The question was whether the confederates, of whom it was now known that they intended to appear at court with a petition, should be admitted or not? The Duke of Arschot, Counts Aremberg, Megen, and Barlaimont gave their negative to the proposition. "What need of five hundred persons," said the latter, "to deliver a small memorial? This paradox of humility and defiance implies no good. Let them send to us one respectable man from among their number without pomp, without assumption, and so submit their application to us. Otherwise, shut the gates upon them, or if some insist on their admission let them be closely watched, and let the first act of insolence which any one of them shall be guilty of be punished with death." In this advice concurred Count Mansfeld, whose own son was among the conspirators; he had even threatened to disinherit his son if he did not quickly abandon the league.

Counts Megen, also, and Aremberg hesitated to receive the petition; the Prince of Orange, however, Counts Egmont, Horn, Hogstraten, and others voted emphatically for it. "The confederates," they declared, "were known to them as men of integrity and honor; a great part of them were connected with themselves by friendship and relationship, and they dared vouch for their behavior. Every subject was allowed to petition; a right which was enjoyed by the meanest individual in the state could not without injustice be denied to so respectable a body of men." It was therefore resolved by a majority of votes to admit the confederates on the condition that they should appear unarmed and conduct themselves temperately. The squabbles of the members of council had occupied the greater part of the sitting, so that it was necessary to adjourn the discussion to the following day. In order that the principal matter in debate might not again be lost sight of in useless complaints the regent at once hastened to the point: "Brederode, we are informed," she said, "is coming to us, with an address in the name of the league, demanding the abolition of the Inquisition and a mitigation of the edicts. The advice of my senate is to guide me in my answer to him; but before you give your opinions on this point permit me to premise a few words. I am told that there are many even amongst yourselves who load the religious edicts of the Emperor, my father, with open reproaches, and describe them to the people as inhuman and barbarous. Now I ask you, lords and gentlemen, knights of the Fleece, counsellors of his majesty and of the state, whether you did not yourselves vote for these edicts, whether the states of the realm have not recognized them as lawful? Why is that now blamed, which was formerly declared right? Is it because they have now become even more necessary than they then were? Since when is the Inquisition a new thing in the Netherlands? Is it not full sixteen years ago since the Emperor established it? And wherein is it more cruel than the edicts? If it be allowed that the latter were the work of wisdom, if the universal consent of the states has sanctioned them— why this opposition to the former, which is nevertheless far more humane than the edicts, if they are to be observed to the letter? Speak now freely; I am not desirous of fettering your decision; but it is your business to see that it is not misled by passion and prejudice." The council of state was again, as it always had been, divided between two opinions; but the few who spoke for the Inquisition and the literal execution of the edicts were outvoted by the opposite party with the Prince of Orange at its head. "Would to heaven," he began,—"that my representations had been then thought worthy of attention, when as yet the grounds of apprehension were remote; things would in that case never have been carried so far as to make recourse to extreme measures indispensable, nor would men have been plunged deeper in error by the very means which were intended to beguile them from their delusion. We are all unanimous on the one main point. We all wish to see the Catholic religion safe; if this end can be secured without the aid of the Inquisition, it is well, and we offer our wealth and our blood to its service; but on this very point it is that our opinions are divided.

"There are two kinds of inquisition: the see of Rome lays claim to one, the other has, from time immemorial, been exercised by the bishops. The force of prejudice and of custom has made the latter light and supportable to us. It will find little opposition in the Netherlands, and the augmented numbers of the bishops will make it effective. To what purpose then insist on the former, the mere name of which is revolting to all the feelings of our minds? When so many nations exist without it why should it be imposed on us? Before Luther appeared it was never heard of; but the troubles with Luther happened at a time when there was an inadequate number of spiritual overseers, and when the few bishops were, moreover, indolent, and the licentiousness of the clergy excluded them from the office of judges. Now all is changed; we now count as many bishops as there are provinces. Why should not the policy of the government adjust itself to the altered circumstances of the times? We want leniency, not severity. The repugnance of the people is manifest — this we must seek to appease if we would not have it burst out into rebellion. With the death of Pius IV. the full powers of the inquisitors have expired; the new pope has as yet sent no ratification of their authority, without which no one formerly ventured to exercise his office. Now, therefore, is the time when it can be suspended without infringing the rights of any party.

"What I have stated with regard to the Inquisition holds equally good in respect to the edicts also. The exigency of the times called them forth, but are not those times passed? So long an experience of them ought at last to have taught us that against hersey no means are less successful than the fagot and sword. What incredible progress has not the new religion made during only the last few years in the provinces; and if we investigate the cause of this increase we shall find it principally in the glorious constancy of those who have fallen sacrifices to the truth of their opinions. Carried away by sympathy and admiration, men begin to weigh in silence whether what is maintained with such invincible courage may not really be the truth. In France and in England the same severities may have been inflicted on the Protestants, but have they been attended with any better success there than here? The very earliest Christians boasted that the blood of the martyrs was the seed of the church. The Emperor Julian, the most terrible enemy that Christianity ever experienced, was fully persuaded of this. Convinced that persecution did but kindle enthusiasm he betook himself to ridicule and derision, and found these weapons far more effective than force. In the Greek empire different teachers of heresy have arisen at different times. Arius under Constantine, Aetius under Constantius, Nestorius under Theodosius. But even against these arch- heretics and their disciples such cruel measures were never resorted to as are thought necessary against our unfortunate country—and yet where are all those sects now which once a whole world, I had almost said, could not contain? This is the natural course of heresy. If it is treated with contempt it crumbles into insignificance. It is as iron, which, if it lies idle, corrodes, and only becomes sharp by use. Let no notice be paid to it, and it loses its most powerful attraction, the magic of what is new and what is forbidden. Why will we not content ourselves with the measures which have been approved of by the wisdom of such great rulers? Example is ever the safest guide.

"But what need to go to pagan antiquity for guidance and example when we have near at hand the glorious precedent of Charles V., the greatest of kings, who taught at last by experience, abandoned the bloody path of persecution, and for many years before his abdication adopted milder measures. And Philip himself, our most gracious sovereign, seemed at first strongly inclined to leniency until the counsels of Granvella and of others like him changed these views; but with what right or wisdom they may settle between themselves. To me, however, it has always appeared indispensable that legislation to be wise and successful must adjust itself to the manners and maxims of the times. In conclusion, I would beg to remind you of the close understanding which subsists between the Huguenots and the Flemish Protestants. Let us beware of exasperating them any further. Let us not act the part of French Catholics towards them, lest they should play the Huguenots against us, and, like the latter, plunge their country into the horrors of a civil war."

> [No one need wonder, says Burgundias (a vehement stickler for the Roman Catholic religion

and the Spanish party), that the speech of this prince evinced so much acquaintance with philosophy; he had acquired it in his intercourse with Balduin. 180. Barry, 174-178. Hopper, 72. Strada, 123,124.]

It was, perhaps, not so much the irresistible truth of his arguments, which, moreover, were supported by a decisive majority in the senate, as rather the ruinous state of the military resources, and the exhaustion of the treasury, that prevented the adoption of the opposite opinion which recommended an appeal to the force of arms that the Prince of Orange had chiefly to thank for the attention which now at last was paid to his representations. In order to avert at first the violence of the storm, and to gain time, which was so necessary to place the government in a better sate of preparation, it was agreed that a portion of the demands should be accorded to the confederates. It was also resolved to mitigate the penal statutes of the Emperor, as he himself would certainly mitigate them, were he again to appear among them at that day —and as, indeed, he had once shown under circumstances very similar to the present that he did not think it derogatory to his high dignity to do. The Inquisition was not to be introduced in any place where it did not already exist, and where it had been it should adopt a milder system, or even be entirely suspended, especially since the inquisitors had not yet been confirmed in their office by the pope. The latter reason was put prominently forward, in order to deprive the Protestants of the gratification of ascribing the concessions to any fear of their own power, or to the justice of their demands. The privy council was commissioned to draw out this decree of the senate without delay. Thus prepared the confederates were awaited.

THE GUEUX.

The members of the senate had not yet dispersed, when all Brussels resounded with the report that the confederates were approaching the town. They consisted of no more than two hundred horse, but rumor greatly exaggerated their numbers. Filled with consternation, the regent consulted with her ministers whether it was best to close the gates on the approaching party or to seek safety in flight? Both suggestions were rejected as dishonorable; and the peaceable entry of the nobles soon allayed all fears of violence. The first morning after their arrival they assembled at Kuilemberg house, where Brederode administered to them a second oath, binding them before all other duties to stand by one another, and even with arms if necessary. At this meeting a letter from Spain was produced, in which it was stated that a certain Protestant, whom, they all knew and valued, had been burned alive in that country by a slow fire. After these and similar preliminaries he called on them one after another by name to take the new oath and renew the old one in their own names and in those of the absent. The next day, the 5th of April, 1556, was fixed for the presentation of the petition. Their numbers now amounted to between three and four hundred. Amongst them were many retainers of the high nobility, as also several servants of the king himself and of the duchess.

With the Counts of Nassau and Brederode at their head, and formed in ranks of four by four, they advanced in procession to the palace; all Brussels attended the unwonted spectacle in silent astonishment. Here were to be seen a body of men advancing with too much boldness and confidence to look like supplicants, and led by two men who were not wont to be petitioners; and, on the other hand, with so much order and stillness as do not usually accompany rebellion. The regent received the procession surrounded by all her counsellors and the Knights of the Fleece. "These noble Netherlanders," thus Brederode respectfully addressed her, "who here present themselves before your highness, wish in their own name, and of many others besides who are shortly to arrive, to present to you a petition of whose importance as well as of their own humility this solemn procession must convince you. I, as speaker of this body, entreat you to receive our petition, which contains nothing but what is in unison with the laws of our country and the honor of the king."

"If this petition," replied Margaret, "really contains nothing which is at variance either with the good of the country, or with the authority of the king, there is no doubt that it will be favorably considered." "They had learnt," continued the spokesman, "with indignation and regret that suspicious objects had been imputed to their association, and that interested parties had endeavored to prejudice her highness against him; they therefore craved that she would name the authors of so grave an accusation, and compel them to bring their charges publicly, and in due form, in order that he who should be found guilty might suffer the punishment of his demerits." "Undoubtedly," replied the regent, "she had received unfavorable rumors of their designs and alliance. She could not be blamed, if in consequence she had thought it requisite to call the attention of the governors of the provinces to the matter; but, as to giving up the names of her informants to betray state secrets," she added, with an appearance of displeasure, "that could not in justice be required of her." She then appointed the next day for answering their petition; and in the meantime she proceeded to consult the members of her council upon it.

"Never" (so ran the petition which, according to some, was drawn up by the celebrated Balduin), "never had they failed in their loyalty to their king, and nothing now could be farther from their hearts; but they would rather run the risk of incurring the displeasure of their sovereign than allow him to remain longer in ignorance of the evils with which their native country was menaced, by the forcible introduction of the Inquisition and the continued enforcement of the edicts. They had long remained consoling themselves with the expectation that a general assembly of the states would be summoned to remedy these grievances; but now that even this hope was extinguished, they held it to be their duty to give timely warning to the regent. They, therefore, entreated her highness to send to Madrid an envoy, well disposed, and fully acquainted with the state and temper of the times, who should endeavor to persuade the king to comply with the demands of the whole nation, and abolish the Inquisition, to revoke the edicts, and in their stead cause new and more humane ones to be drawn up at a general assembly of the states. But, in the meanwhile, until they could learn the king's decision, they prayed that the edicts and the operations of the Inquisition be suspended." "If," they concluded, "no attention should be paid to their humble request, they took God, the king, the regent, and all her counsellors to witness that they had done their part, and were not responsible for any unfortunate result that might happen."

The following day the confederates, marching in the same order of procession, but in still greater numbers (Counts Bergen and Kuilemberg having, in the interim, joined them with their adherents), appeared before the regent in order to receive her answer. It was written on the margin of the petition, and was to the effect, "that entirely to suspend the Inquisition and the edicts, even temporarily, was beyond her powers; but in compliance with the wishes of the confederates she was ready to despatch one of the nobles to the king in Spain, and also to support their petition with all her influence. In the meantime, she would recommend the inquisitors to administer their office with moderation; but in return she should expect on the part of the league that they should abstain from all acts of violence, and undertake nothing to the prejudice of the Catholic faith." Little as these vague and general promises satisfied the confederates, they were, nevertheless, as much as they could have reasonably expected to gain at first. The granting or refusing of the petition had nothing to do with the primary object of the league. Enough for them at present that it was once recognized, enough that it was now, as it were, an established body, which by its power and threats might, if necessary, overawe the government. The confederates, therefore, acted quite consistently with their designs, in contenting themselves with this answer, and referring the rest to the good pleasure of the king. As, indeed, the whole pantomime of petitioning had only been invented to cover the more daring plan of the league, until it should have strength enough to show itself in its true light, they felt that much more depended on their being able to continue this mask, and on the favorable reception of their petition, than on its speedily being granted. In a new memorial, which they delivered three days after, they pressed for an express testimonial from the regent that they had done no more than their duty, and been guided simply by their zeal for the service of the king. When the duchess evaded a declaration, they even sent a person to repeat this request in a private interview. "Time alone and their future behavior," she replied to this person, "would enable her to judge of their designs."

The league had its origin in banquets, and a banquet gave it form and perfection. On the very day that the second petition was presented Brederode entertained the confederates in Kuilemberg house. About three hundred guests assembled; intoxication gave them courage, and their audacity rose with their numbers. During the conversation one of their number happened to remark that he had overheard the Count of Barlaimont whisper in French to the regent, who was seen to turn pale on the delivery of the petitions, that "she need not be afraid of a band of beggars (gueux);" (in fact, the majority of them had by their bad management of their incomes only too well deserved this appellation.) Now, as the very name for their fraternity was the very thing which had most perplexed them, an expression was eagerly caught up, which, while it cloaked the presumption of their enterprise in humility, was at the same time appropriate to them as petitioners. Immediately they drank to one another under this name, and the cry "long live the Gueux!" was accompanied with a general shout of applause. After the cloth had been removed Brederode appeared with a wallet over his shoulder similar to that which the vagrant pilgrims and mendicant monks of the time used to carry, and after returning thanks to all for their accession to the league, and boldly assuring them that he was ready to venture life and limb for every individual present, he drank to the health of the whole company out of a wooden beaker. The cup went round and every one uttered the same vow as be set it to his lips. Then one after the other they received the beggar's purse, and each hung it on a nail which he had appropriated to himself. The shouts and uproar attending this buffoonery attracted the Prince of Orange and Counts Egmont and Horn, who by chance were passing the spot at the very moment, and on entering the house were boisterously pressed by Brederode, as host, to remain and drink a glass with them.

> ["But," Egmont asserted in his written defence
> "we drank only one single small glass, and there-
> upon they cried 'long live the king and the Gueux!'

This was the first time that I heard that appellation, and it certainly did not please me. But the times were so bad that one was often compelled to share in much that was against one's inclination, and I knew not but I was doing an innocent thing." Proces criminels des Comtes d'Egmont, etc.. 7. 1. Egmont's defence, Hopper, 94. Strada, 127-130. Burgund., 185, 187.]

The entrance of three such influential personages renewed the mirth of the guests, and their festivities soon passed the bounds of moderation. Many were intoxicated; guests and attendants mingled together without distinction; the serious and the ludicrous, drunken fancies and affairs of state were blended one with another in a burlesque medley; and the discussions on the general distress of the country ended in the wild uproar of a bacchanalian revel. But it did not stop here; what they had resolved on in the moment of intoxication they attempted when sober to carry into execution. It was necessary to manifest to the people in some striking shape the existence of their protectors, and likewise to fan the zeal of the faction by a visible emblem; for this end nothing could be better than to adopt publicly this name of Gueux, and to borrow from it the tokens of the association. In a few days the town of Brussels swarmed with ash-gray garments such as were usually worn by mendicant friars and penitents. Every confederate put his whole family and domestics in this dress. Some carried wooden bowls thinly overlaid with plates of silver, cups of the same kind, and wooden knives; in short the whole paraphernalia of the beggar tribe, which they either fixed around their hats or suspended from their girdles: Round the neck they wore a golden or silver coin, afterwards called the Geusen penny, of which one side bore the effigy of the king, with the inscription, "True to the king;" on the other side were seen two hands folded together holding a wallet, with the words "as far as the beggar's scrip." Hence the origin of the name "Gueux," which was subsequently borne in the Netherlands by all who seceded from popery and took up arms against the king.

Before the confederates separated and dispersed among the provinces they presented themselves once more before the duchess, in order to remind her of the necessity of leniency towards the heretics until the arrival of the king's answer from Spain, if she did not wish to drive the people to extremities. "If, however," they added, "a contrary behavior should give rise to any evils they at least must be regarded as having done their duty."

To this the regent replied, "she hoped to be able to adopt such measures as would render it impossible for disorders to ensue; but if, nevertheless, they did occur, she could ascribe them to no one but the confederates. She therefore earnestly admonished them on their part to fulfil their engagements, but especially to receive no new members into the league, to hold no more private assemblies, and generally not to attempt any novel and unconstitutional measures." And in order to tranquillize their minds she commanded her private secretary, Berti, to show them the letters to the inquisitors and secular judges, wherein they were enjoined to observe moderation towards all those who had not aggravated their heretical offences by any civil crime. Before their departure from Brussels they named four presidents from among their number who were to take care of the affairs of the league, and also particular administrators for each province. A few were left behind in Brussels to keep a watchful eye on all the movements of the court. Brederode, Kuilemberg, and Bergen at last quitted the town, attended by five hundred and fifty horsemen, saluted it once more beyond the walls with a discharge of musketry, and then the three leaders parted, Brederode taking the road to Antwerp, and the two others to Guelders. The regent had sent off an express to Antwerp to warn the magistrate of that town against him. On his arrival more than a thousand persons thronged to the hotel where he had taken up his abode. Showing himself at a window, with a full wineglass in his hand, he thus addressed them: "Citizens of Antwerp! I am here at the hazard of my life and my property to relieve you from the oppressive burden of the Inquisition. If you are ready to share this enterprise with me, and to acknowledge me as your leader, accept the health which I here drink to you, and hold up your hands in testimony of your approbation." Hereupon he drank to their health, and all hands were raised amidst clamorous shouts of exultation. After this heroic deed he quitted Antwerp.

Immediately after the delivery of the "petition of the nobles," the regent had caused a new form of the edicts to be drawn up in the privy council, which should keep the mean between the commands of the king and the demands of the confederates. But the next question that arose was to determine whether it would be advisable immediately to promulgate this mitigated form, or moderation, as it was commonly called, or to submit it first to the king for his ratification. The privy council who maintained that it would be presumptuous to take a step so important and so contrary to the declared sentiments of the monarch without having first obtained his sanction, opposed the vote of the Prince of Orange who supported the former proposition. Besides, they urged, there was cause to fear that it would not even content the nation.

A "moderation" devised with the assent of the states was what they particularly insisted on. In order, therefore, to gain the consent of the states, or rather to obtain it from them by stealth, the regent artfully propounded the question to the provinces singly, and first of all to those which possessed the least freedom, such as Artois, Namur, and Luxemburg. Thus she not only prevented one province encouraging another in opposition, but also gained this advantage by it, that the freer provinces, such as Flanders and Brabant, which were prudently reserved to the last, allowed themselves to be carried away by the example of the others. By a very illegal procedure the representatives of the towns were taken by surprise, and their consent exacted before they could confer with their constituents, while complete silence was imposed upon them with regard to the whole transaction. By these means the regent obtained the unconditional consent of some of the provinces to the "moderation," and, with a few slight changes, that of other provinces. Luxemburg and Namur subscribed it without scruple. The states of Artois simply added the condition that false informers should be subjected to a retributive penalty; those of Hainault demanded that instead of confiscation of the estates, which directly militated against their privileges, another discretionary punishment should be introduced. Flanders called for the entire abolition of the Inquisition, and desired that the accused might be secured in right of appeal to their own province. The states of Brabant were outwitted by the intrigues of the court. Zealand, Holland, Utrecht, Guelders, and Friesland as being provinces which enjoyed the most important privileges, and which, moreover, watched over them with the greatest jealousy, were never asked for their opinion. The provincial courts of judicature had also been required to make a report on the projected amendment of the law, but we may well suppose that it was unfavorable, as it never reached Spain. From the principal cause of this "moderation," which, however, really deserved its name, we may form a judgment of the general character of the edicts themselves. "Sectarian writers," it ran, "the heads and teachers of sects, as also those who conceal heretical meetings, or cause any other public scandal, shall be punished with the gallows, and their estates, where the law of the province permit it, confiscated; but if they abjure their errors, their punishment shall be commuted into decapitation with the sword, and their effects shall be preserved to their families." A cruel snare for parental affection! Less grievous heretics, it was further enacted, shall, if penitent, be pardoned; and if impenitent shall be compelled to leave the country, without, however, forfeiting their estates, unless by continuing to lead others astray they deprive themselves of the benefit of this provision. The Anabaptists, however, were expressly excluded from benefiting by this clause; these, if they did not clear themselves by the most thorough repentance, were to forfeit their possessions; and if, on the other hand, they relapsed after penitence, that is, were backsliding heretics, they were to be put to death without mercy. The greater regard for life and property which is observable in this ordinance as compared with the edicts, and which we might be tempted to ascribe to a change of intention in the Spanish ministry, was nothing more than a compulsory step extorted by the determined opposition of the nobles. So little, too, were the people in the Netherlands satisfied by this "moderation," which fundamentally did not remove a single abuse, that instead of "moderation" (mitigation), they indignantly called it "moorderation," that is, murdering.

After the consent of the states had in this manner been extorted from them, the "moderation" was submitted to the council of the state, and, after receiving their signatures, forwarded to the king in Spain in order to receive from his ratification the force of law.

The embassy to Madrid, which had been agreed upon with the confederates, was at the outset entrusted to the Marquis of Bergen, who, however, from a distrust of the present disposition of the king, which was only too well grounded, and from reluctance to engage alone in so delicate a business, begged for a coadjutor.

> [This Marquis of Bergen is to be distinguished from Count William of Bergen, who was among the first who subscribed the covenant. Vigi. ad Hopper, Letter VII.]

He obtained one in the Baron of Montigny, who had previously been employed in a similar duty, and had discharged it with high credit. As, however, circumstances had since altered so much that he had just anxiety as to his present reception in Madrid for his greater safety, he stipulated with the duchess that she should write to the monarch previously; and that he, with his companion, should, in the meanwhile, travel slowly enough to give time for the king's answer reaching him en route. His good genius wished, as it appeared, to save him from the terrible fate which awaited him in Madrid, for his departure was delayed by an unexpected obstacle, the Marquis of Bergen being disabled from setting out immediately through a wound which he received from the blow of a tennis-ball. At last, however, yielding to the pressing importunities of the regent, who was anxious to expedite the business, he set out alone, not, as he hoped, to carry the cause of his nation, but to die for it.

In the meantime the posture of affairs had changed so greatly in the Netherlands, the step which the nobles had recently taken had so nearly brought on a complete rupture with the government, that it seemed impossible for the Prince of Orange and his friends to maintain any longer the intermediate and delicate position which they had hitherto held between the country and the court, or to reconcile the contradictory duties to which it gave rise. Great must have been the restraint which, with their mode of thinking, they had to put on themselves not to take part in this contest; much, too, must their natural love of liberty, their patriotism, and their principles of toleration have suffered from the constraint which their official station imposed upon them. On the other hand, Philip's distrust, the little regard which now for a long time had been paid to their advice, and the marked slights which the duchess publicly put upon them, had greatly contributed to cool their zeal for the service, and to render irksome the longer continuance of a part which they played with so much repugnance and with so little thanks. This feeling was strengthened by several intimations they received from Spain which placed beyond doubt the great displeasure of the king at the petition of the nobles, and his little satisfaction with their own behavior on that occasion, while they were also led to expect that he was about to enter upon measures, to which, as favorable to the liberties of their country, and for the most part friends or blood relations of the confederates; they could never lend their countenance or support. On the name which should be applied in Spain to the confederacy of the nobles it principally depended what course they should follow for the future. If the petition should be called rebellion no alternative would be left them but either to come prematurely to a dangerous explanation with the court, or to aid it in treating as enemies those with whom they had both a fellow-feeling and a common interest. This perilous alternative could only be avoided by withdrawing entirely from public affairs; this plan they had once before practically adopted, and under present circumstances it was something more than a simple expedient. The whole nation had their eyes upon them. An unlimited confidence in their integrity, and the universal veneration for their persons, which closely bordered on idolatry, would ennoble the cause which they might make their own and ruin that which they should abandon. Their share in the administration of the state, though it were nothing more than nominal, kept the opposite party in check; while they attended the senate violent measures were avoided because their continued presence still favored some expectations of succeeding by gentle means. The withholding of their approbation, even if it did not proceed from their hearts, dispirited the faction, which, on the contrary, would exert its full strength so soon as it could reckon even distantly on obtaining so weighty a sanction. The very measures of the government which, if they came through their hands, were certain of a favorable reception and issue, would without them prove suspected and futile; even the royal concessions, if they were not obtained by the mediation of these friends of the people, would fail of the chief part of their efficacy. Besides, their retirement from public affairs would deprive the regent of the benefit of their advice at a time when counsel was most indispensable to her; it would, moreover, leave the preponderance with a party which, blindly dependent on the court, and ignorant of the peculiarities of republican character, would neglect nothing to aggravate the evil, and to drive to extremity the already exasperated mind of the public.

All these motives (and it is open to every one, according to his good or bad opinion of the prince, to say which was the most influential) tended alike to move him to desert the regent, and to divest himself of all share in public affairs. An opportunity for putting this resolve into execution soon presented itself. The prince had voted for the immediate promulgation of the newly-revised edicts; but the regent, following the suggestion of her privy council, had determined to transmit them first to the king. "I now see clearly," he broke out with well-acted vehemence, "that all the advice which I give is distrusted. The king requires no servants whose loyalty he is determined to doubt; and far be it from me to thrust my services upon a sovereign who is unwilling to receive them. Better, therefore, for him and me that I withdraw from public affairs." Count Horn expressed himself nearly to the same effect. Egmont requested permission to visit the baths of Aix-la- Chapelle, the use of which had been prescribed to him by his physician, although (as it is stated in his accusation) he appeared health itself. The regent, terrified at the consequences which must inevitably follow this step, spoke sharply to the prince. "If neither my representations, nor the general welfare can prevail upon you, so far as to induce you to relinquish this intention, let me advise you to be more careful, at least, of your own reputation. Louis of Nassau is your brother; he and Count Brederode, the heads of the confederacy, have publicly been your guests. The petition is in substance identical with your own representations in the council of state. If you now suddenly desert the cause of your king will it not be universally said that you favor the conspiracy?" We do not find it anywhere stated whether the prince really withdrew at this time from the council of state; at all events, if he did, he must soon have altered his mind, for shortly after he appears again in public transactions. Egmont allowed himself to be overcome by the remonstrances of the regent; Horn alone actually withdrew himself to one of his estates, — [Where be remained three months inactive.] — with the resolution of never more serving either emperor or king. Meanwhile the Gueux had dispersed themselves through the provinces, and spread everywhere the most favorable reports of their success. According to their assertions, religious freedom was finally assured; and in order to confirm their statements they helped themselves, where the truth failed, with falsehood. For example, they produced a forged letter of the Knights of the Fleece, in which the latter were made solemnly to declare that for the future no one need fear imprisonment, or banishment, or death on account of religion, unless he also committed a political crime; and even in that case the confederates alone were to be his judges; and this regulation was to be in force until the king, with the consent and advice of the states of the realm, should otherwise dispose. Earnestly as the knights applied themselves upon the first information of the fraud to rescue the nation from their delusion, still it had already in this short interval done good service to the faction. If there are truths whose effect is limited to a single instant, then inventions which last so long can easily assume their place. Besides, the report, however false, was calculated both to awaken distrust between the regent and the knights, and to support the courage of the Protestants by fresh hopes, while it also furnished those who were meditating innovation an appearance of right, which, however unsubstantial they themselves knew it to be, served as a colorable pretext for their proceedings. Quickly as this delusion was dispelled, still, in the short space of time that it obtained belief, it had occasioned so many extravagances, had introduced so much irregularity and license, that a return to the former state of things became impossible, and continuance in the course already commenced was rendered necessary as well by habit as by despair. On the very first news of this happy result the fugitive Protestants had returned to their homes, which they had so unwillingly abandoned; those who had been in concealment came forth from their hiding-places; those who had hitherto paid homage to the new religion in their hearts alone, emboldened by these pretended acts of toleration, now gave in their adhesion to it publicly and decidedly. The name of the "Gueux" was extolled in all the provinces; they were called the pillars of religion and liberty; their party increased daily, and many of the merchants began to wear their insignia. The latter made an alteration in the "Gueux" penny, by introducing two travellers' staffs, laid crosswise, to intimate that they stood prepared and ready at any instant to forsake house and hearth for the sake of religion. The Gueux league, in short, had now given to things an entirely different form. The murmurs of the people, hitherto impotent and despised, as being the cries of individuals, had, now that they were concentrated, become formidable; and had gained power, direction, and firmness through union. Every one who was rebelliously disposed now looked on himself as the member of a venerable and powerful body, and believed that by carrying his own complaints to the general stock of discontent he secured the free expression of them. To be called an important acquisition to the league flattered the vain; to be lost, unnoticed, and irresponsible in the crowd was an inducement to the timid. The face which the confederacy showed to the nation was very unlike that which it had turned to the court. But had its objects been the purest, had it really been as well disposed towards the throne as it wished to appear, still the multitude would have regarded only what was illegal in its proceedings, and upon them its better intentions would have been entirely lost.

PUBLIC PREACHING.

No moment could be more favorable to the Huguenots and the German Protestants than the present to seek a market for their dangerous commodity in the Netherlands. Accordingly, every considerable town now swarmed with suspicious arrivals, masked spies, and the apostles of every description of heresy. Of the religious parties, which had sprung up by secession from the ruling church, three chiefly had made considerable progress in the provinces. Friesland and the adjoining districts were overrun by the Anabaptists, who, however, as the most indigent, without organization and government, destitute of military resources, and moreover at strife amongst themselves, awakened the least apprehension. Of far more importance were the Calvanists, who prevailed in the southern provinces, and above all in Flanders, who were powerfully supported by their neighbors the Huguenots, the republic of Geneva, the Swiss Cantons, and part of Germany, and whose opinions, with the exception of a slight difference, were also held by the throne in England. They were also the most numerous party, especially among the merchants and common citizens. The Huguenots, expelled from France, had been the chief disseminators of the tenets of this party. The Lutherans were inferior both in numbers and wealth, but derived weight from having many adherents among the nobility. They occupied, for the most part, the eastern portion of the Netherlands, which borders on Germany, and were also to be found in some of the northern territories. Some of the most powerful princes of Germany were their allies; and the religious freedom of that empire, of which by the Burgundian treaty the Netherlands formed an integral part, was claimed by them with some appearance of right. These three religious denominations met together in Antwerp, where the crowded population concealed them, and the mingling of all nations favored liberty. They had nothing in common, except an equally inextinguishable hatred of popery, of the Inquisition in particular, and of the Spanish government, whose instrument it was; while, on the other hand, they watched each other with a jealousy which kept their zeal in exercise, and prevented the glowing ardor of fanaticism from waxing dull.

The regent, in expectation that the projected "moderation" would be sanctioned by the king, had, in the meantime, to gratify the Gueux, recommended the governors and municipal officers of the provinces to be as moderate as possible in their proceedings against heretics; instructions which were eagerly followed, and interpreted in the widest sense by the majority, who had hitherto administered the painful duty of punishment with extreme repugnance. Most of the chief magistrates were in their hearts averse to the Inquisition and the Spanish tyranny, and many were even secretly attached to one or other of the religious parties; even the others were unwilling to inflict punishment on their countrymen to gratify their sworn enemies, the Spaniards. All, therefore, purposely misunderstood the regent, and allowed the Inquisition and the edicts to fall almost entirely into disuse. This forbearance of the government, combined with the brilliant representations of the Gueux, lured from their obscurity the Protestants, who, however, had now grown too powerful to be any longer concealed. Hitherto they had contented themselves with secret assemblies by night; now they thought themselves numerous and formidable enough to venture to these meetings openly and publicly. This license commenced somewhere between Oudenarde and Ghent, and soon spread through the rest of Flanders. A certain Herrnann Stricker, born at Overyssel, formerly a monk, a daring enthusiast of able mind, imposing figure, and ready tongue, was the first who collected the people for a sermon in the open air. The novelty of the thing gathered together a crowd of about seven thousand persons. A magistrate of the neighborhood, more courageous than wise, rushed amongst the crowd with his drawn sword, and attempted to seize the preacher, but was so roughly handled by the multitude, who for want of other weapons took up stones and felled him to the ground, that he was glad to beg for his life.

> [The unheard-of foolhardiness of a single man
> rushing into the midst of a fanatical crowd of sev-
> en thousand people to seize before their eyes one
> whom they adored, proves, more than all that can
> be said on the subject the insolent contempt with

which the Roman Catholics of the time looked
down upon the so-called heretics as an inferior
race of beings.]

This success of the first attempt inspired courage for a second. In the vicinity of Aalst they assembled again in still greater numbers; but on this occasion they provided themselves with rapiers, fire-arms, and halberds, placed sentries at all the approaches, which they also barricaded with carts and carriages. All passers-by were obliged, whether willing or otherwise, to take part in the religious service, and to enforce this object lookout parties were posted at certain distances round the place of meeting. At the entrance booksellers stationed themselves, offering for sale Protestant cate-chisms, religious tracts, and pasquinades on the bishops. The preacher, Hermann Stricker, held forth from a pulpit which was hastily constructed for the occasion out of carts and trunks of trees. A canvas awning drawn over it protected him from the sun and the rain; the preacher's position was in the quarter of the wind that the people might not lose any part of his sermon, which consisted prin-cipally of revilings against popery. Here the sacraments were ad-ministered after the Calvinistic fashion, and water was procured from the nearest river to baptize infants without further ceremony, after the practice, it was pretended, of the earliest times of Christi-anity. Couples were also united in wedlock, and the marriage ties dissolved between others. To be present at this meeting half the population of Ghent had left its gates; their example was soon fol-lowed in other parts, and ere long spread over the whole of East Flanders. In like manner Peter Dathen, another renegade monk, from Poperingen, stirred up West Flanders; as many as fifteen thou-sand persons at a time attended his preaching from the villages and hamlets; their number made them bold, and they broke into the prisons, where some Anabaptists were reserved for martyrdom. In Tournay the Protestants were excited to a similar pitch of daring by Ambrosius Ville, a French Calvinist. They demanded the release of the prisoners of their sect, and repeatedly threatened if their de-mands were not complied with to deliver up the town to the French. It was entirely destitute of a garrison, for the commandant, from fear of treason, had withdrawn it into the castle, and the soldiers, moreover, refused to act against their fellow-citizens. The sectarians carried their audacity to such great lengths as to require one of the churches within the town to be assigned to them; and when this was refused they entered into a league with Valenciennes and Antwerp to obtain a legal recognition of their worship, after the example of the other towns, by open force. These three towns maintained a close connection with each other, and the Protestant party was equally powerful in all. While, however, no one would venture singly to commence the disturbance, they agreed simultaneously to make a beginning with public preaching. Brederode's appearance in Antwerp at last gave them courage. Six thousand persons, men and women, poured forth from the town on an appointed day, on which the same thing happened in Tournay and Valenciennes. The place of meeting was closed in with a line of vehicles, firmly fastened together, and behind them armed men were secretly posted, with a view to protect the service from any surprise. Of the preachers, most of whom were men of the very lowest class — some were Germans, some were Huguenots — and spoke in the Walloon dialect; some even of the citizens felt themselves called upon to take a part in this sacred work, now that no fears of the officers of justice alarmed them. Many were drawn to the spot by mere curiosity to hear what kind of new and unheard-of doctrines these foreign teachers, whose arrival had caused so much talk, would set forth. Others were attracted by the melody of the psalms, which were sung in a French version, after the custom in Geneva. A great number came to hear these sermons as so many amusing comedies such was the buffoonery with which the pope, the fathers of the ecclesiastical council of Trent, purgatory, and other dogmas of the ruling church were abused in them. And, in fact, the more extravagant was this abuse and ridicule the more it tickled the ears of the lower orders; and a universal clapping of hands, as in a theatre, rewarded the speaker who had surpassed others in the wildness of his jokes and denunciations. But the ridicule which was thus cast upon the ruling church was, nevertheless, not entirely lost on the minds of the hearers, as neither were the few grains of truth or reason which occasionally slipped in among it; and many a one, who had sought from these sermons anything but conviction, unconsciously carried away a little also of it.

These assemblies were several times repeated, and each day augmented the boldness of the sectarians; till at last they even ventured, after concluding the service to conduct their preachers home in triumph, with an escort of armed horsemen, and ostentatiously to brave the law. The town council sent express after express to the duchess, entreating her to visit them in person, and if possible to reside for a short time in Antwerp, as the only expedient to curb the arrogance of the populace; and assuring her that the most eminent merchants, afraid of being plundered, were already preparing to quit it. Fear of staking the royal dignity on so hazardous a stroke of policy forbade her compliance; but she despatched in her stead Count Megen, in order to treat with the magistrate for the introduction of a garrison. The rebellious mob, who quickly got an inkling of the object of his visit, gathered around him with tumultuous cries, shouting, "He was known to them as a sworn enemy of the Gueux; that it was notorious he was bringing upon them prisons and the Inquisition, and that he should leave the town instantly." Nor was the tumult quieted till Megen was beyond the gates. The Calvinists now handed in to the magistrate a memorial, in which they showed that their great numbers made it impossible for them henceforward to assemble in secrecy, and requested a separate place of worship to be allowed them inside the town. The town council renewed its entreaties to the duchess to assist, by her personal presence, their perplexities, or at least to send to them the Prince of Orange, as the only person for whom the people still had any respect, and, moreover, as specially bound to the town of Antwerp by his hereditary title of its burgrave. In order to escape the greater evil she was compelled to consent to the second demand, however much against her inclination to entrust Antwerp to the prince. After allowing himself to be long and fruitlessly entreated, for he had all at once resolved to take no further share in public affairs, he yielded at last to the earnest persuasions of the regent and the boisterous wishes of the people. Brederode, with a numerous retinue, came half a mile out of the town to meet him, and both parties saluted each other with a discharge of pistols. Antwerp appeared to have poured out all her inhabitants to welcome her deliverer. The high road swarmed with multitudes; the roofs were taken off the houses in order that they might accommodate more spectators; behind fences, from church-yard walls, even out of graves started up men. The attachment of the people to the prince showed itself in childish effusions. "Long live the Gueux!" was the shout with which young and old received him. "Behold," cried others, "the man who shall give us liberty." "He brings us," cried the Lutherans, "the Confession of Augsburg!" "We don't want the Gueux now!" exclaimed others; "we have no more need of the troublesome journey to Brussels. He alone is everything to us!" Those who knew not what to say vented their extravagant joy in psalms, which they vociferously chanted as they moved along. He, however, maintained his gravity, beckoned for silence, and at last, when no one would listen to him, exclaimed with indignation, half real and half affected, "By God, they ought to consider what they did, or they would one day repent what they had now done." The shouting increased even as he rode into the town. The first conference of the prince with the heads of the different religious sects, whom he sent for and separately interrogated, presently convinced him that the chief source of the evil was the mutual distrust of the several parties, and the suspicions which the citizens entertained of the designs of the government, and that therefore it must be his first business to restore confidence among them all. First of all he attempted, both by persuasion and artifice, to induce the Calvinists, as the most numerous body, to lay down their weapons, and in this he at last, with much labor, succeeded. When, however, some wagons were soon afterwards seen laden with ammunition in Malines, and the high bailiff of Brabant showed himself frequently in the neighborhood of Antwerp with an armed force, the Calvinists, fearing hostile interruption of their religious worship, besought the prince to allot them a place within the walls for their sermons, which should be secure from a surprise. He succeeded once more in pacifying them, and his presence fortunately prevented an outbreak on the Assumption of the Virgin, which, as usual, had drawn a crowd to the town, and from whose sentiments there was but too much reason for alarm. The image of the Virgin was, with the usual pomp, carried round the town without interruption; a few words of abuse, and a suppressed murmur about idolatry, was all that the disapproving multitudes indulged in against the procession.

1566. While the regent received from one province after another the most melancholy accounts of the excesses of the Protestants, and while she trembled for Antwerp, which she was compelled to leave in the dangerous hands of the Prince of Orange, a new terror assailed her from another quarter. Upon the first authentic tidings of the public preaching she immediately called upon the league to fulfil its promises and to assist her in restoring order. Count Brederode used this pretext to summon a general meeting of the whole league, for which he could not have selected a more dangerous moment than the present. So ostentatious a display of the strength of the league, whose existence and protection had alone encouraged the Protestant mob to go the length it had already gone, would now raise the confidence of the sectarians, while in the same degree it depressed the courage of the regent. The convention took place in the town of Liege St. Truyen, into which Brederode and Louis of Nassau had thrown themselves at the head of two thousand confederates. As the long delay of the royal answer from Madrid seemed to presage no good from that quarter, they considered it advisable in any case to extort from the regent a letter of indemnity for their persons.

Those among them who were conscious of a disloyal sympathy with the Protestant mob looked on its licentiousness as a favorable circumstance for the league; the apparent success of those to whose degrading fellowship they had deigned to stoop led them to alter their tone; their former laudable zeal began to degenerate into insolence and defiance. Many thought that they ought to avail themselves of the general confusion and the perplexity of the duchess to assume a bolder tone and heap demand upon demand. The Roman Catholic members of the league, among whom many were in their hearts still strongly inclined to the royal cause, and who had been drawn into a connection with the league by occasion and example, rather than from feeling and conviction, now heard to their astonishment propositions for establishing universal freedom of religion, and were not a little shocked to discover in how perilous an enterprise they had hastily implicated themselves. On this discovery the young Count Mansfeld withdrew immediately from it, and internal dissensions already began to undermine the work of precipitation and haste, and imperceptibly to loosen the joints of the league.

Count Egmont and William of Orange were empowered by the regent to treat with the confederates. Twelve of the latter, among whom were Louis of Nassau, Brederode, and Kuilemberg, conferred with them in Duffle, a village near Malines. "Wherefore this new step?" demanded the regent by the mouth of these two noblemen. "I was required to despatch ambassadors to Spain; and I sent them. The edicts and the Inquisition were complained of as too rigorous; I have rendered both more lenient. A general assembly of the states of the realm was proposed; I have submitted this request to the king because I could not grant it from my own authority. What, then, have I unwittingly either omitted or done that should render necessary this assembling in St. Truyen? Is it perhaps fear of the king's anger and of its consequences that disturbs the confederates? The provocation certainly is great, but his mercy is even greater. Where now is the promise of the league to excite no disturbances amongst the people? Where those high-sounding professions that they were ready to die at my feet rather, than offend against any of the prerogatives of the crown? The innovators already venture on things which border closely on rebellion, and threaten the state with destruction; and it is to the league that they appeal. If it continues silently to tolerate this it will justly bring on itself the charge of participating in the guilt of their offences; if it is honestly disposed towards the sovereign it cannot remain longer inactive in this licentiousness of the mob. But, in truth, does it not itself outstrip the insane population by its dangerous example, concluding, as it is known to do, alliances with the enemies of the country, and confirming the evil report of its designs by the present illegal meeting?"

Against these reproaches the league formally justified itself in a memorial which it deputed three of its members to deliver to the council of state at Brussels.

"All," it commenced, "that your highness has done in respect to our petition we have felt with the most lively gratitude; and we cannot complain of any new measure, subsequently adopted, inconsistent with your promise; but we cannot help coming to the conclusion that the orders of your highness are by the judicial courts, at least, very little regarded; for we are continually hearing—and our own eyes attest to the truth of the report—that in all quarters our fellow-citizens are in spite of the orders of your highness still mercilessly dragged before the courts of justice and condemned to death for religion. What the league engaged on its part to do it has honestly fulfilled; it has, too, to the utmost of its power endeavored to prevent the public preachings; but it certainly is no wonder if the long delay of an answer from Madrid fills the mind of the people with distrust, and if the disappointed hopes of a general assembly of the states disposes them to put little faith in any further assurances. The league has never allied, nor ever felt any temptation to ally, itself with the enemies of the country. If the arms of France were to appear in the provinces we, the confederates, would be the first to mount and drive them back again. The league, however, desires to be candid with your highness. We thought we read marks of displeasure in your countenance; we see men in exclusive possession of your favor who are notorious for their hatred against us. We daily hear that persons are warned from associating with us, as with those infected with the plague, while we are denounced with the arrival of the king as with the opening of a day of judgment—what is more natural than that such distrust shown to us should at last rouse our own? That the attempt to blacken our league with the reproach of treason, that the warlike preparations of the Duke of Savoy and of other princes, which, according to common report, are directed against ourselves; the negotiations of the king with the French court to obtain a passage through that kingdom for a Spanish army, which is destined, it is said, for the Netherlands—what wonder if these and similar occurrences should have stimulated us to think in time of the means of self-defence, and to strengthen ourselves by an alliance with our friends beyond the frontier? On a general, uncertain, and vague rumor we are accused of a share in this licentiousness of the Protestant mob; but who is safe from general rumor? True it is, certainly, that of our numbers some are Protestants, to whom religious toleration would be a welcome boon; but even they have never forgotten what they owe to their sovereign. It is not fear of the king's anger which instigated us to hold this assembly. The king is good, and we still hope that he is also just. It cannot, therefore, be pardon that we seek from him, and just as little can it be oblivion that we solicit for our actions, which are far from being the least considerable of the services we have at different times rendered his majesty. Again, it is true, that the delegates of the Lutherans and Calvinists are with us in St. Truyen; nay, more, they have delivered to us a petition which, annexed to this memorial, we here present to your highness. In it they offer to go unarmed to their preachings if the league will tender its security to them, and be willing to engage for a general meeting of the states. We have thought it incumbent upon us to communicate both these matters to you, for our guarantee can have no force unless it is at the same time confirmed by your highness and some of your principal counsellors. Among these no one can be so well acquainted with the circumstances of our cause, or be so upright in intention towards us, as the Prince of Orange and Counts Horn and Egmont. We gladly accept these three as meditators if the necessary powers are given to them, and assurance is afforded us that no troops will be enlisted without their knowledge. This guarantee, however, we only require for a given period, before the expiration of which it will rest with the king whether he will cancel or confirm it for the future. If the first should be his will it will then be but fair that time should be allowed us to place our persons and our property in security; for this three weeks will be sufficient. Finally, and in conclusion, we on our part also pledge ourselves to undertake nothing new without the concurrence of those three persons, our mediators."

The league would not have ventured to hold such bold language if it had not reckoned on powerful support and protection; but the regent was as little in a condition to concede their demands as she was incapable of vigorously opposing them. Deserted in Brussels by most of her counsellors of state, who had either departed to their provinces, or under some pretext or other had altogether withdrawn from public affairs; destitute as well of advisers as of money (the latter want had compelled her, in the first instance, to appeal to the liberality of the clergy; when this proved insufficient, to have recourse to a lottery), dependent on orders from Spain, which were ever expected and never received, she was at last reduced to the degrading expedient of entering into a negotiation with the confederates in St. Truyen, that they should wait twenty-four days longer for the king's resolution before they took any further steps. It was certainly surprising that the king still continued to delay a decisive answer to the petition, although it was universally known that he had answered letters of a much later date, and that the regent earnestly importuned him on this head. She had also, on the commencement of the public preaching, immediately despatched the Marquis of Bergen after the Baron of Montigny, who, as an eye-witness of these new occurrences, could confirm her written statements, to move the king to an earlier decision.

1566. In the meanwhile, the Flemish ambassador, Florence of Montigny, had arrived in Madrid, where he was received with a great show of consideration. His instructions were to press for the abolition of the Inquisition and the mitigation of the edicts; the augmentation of the council of state, and the incorporation with it of the two other councils; the calling of a general assembly of the states, and, lastly, to urge the solicitations of the regent for a personal visit from the king. As the latter, however, was only desirous of gaining time, Montigny was put off with fair words until the arrival of his coadjutor, without whom the king was not willing to come to any final determination. In the meantime, Montigny had every day and at any hour that he desired, an audience with the king, who also commanded that on all occasions the despatches of the duchess and the answers to them should be communicated to himself. He was, too, frequently admitted to the council for Belgian affairs, where he never omitted to call the king's attention to the necessity of a general assembly of the states, as being the only means of successfully meeting the troubles which had arisen, and as likely to supersede the necessity of any other measure. He moreover impressed upon him that a general and unreserved indemnity for the past would alone eradicate the distrust, which was the source of all existing complaints, and would always counteract the good effects of every measure, however well advised. He ventured, from a thorough acquaintance with circumstances and accurate knowledge of the character of his countrymen, to pledge himself to the king for their inviolable loyalty, as soon as they should be convinced of the honesty of his intentions by the straightforwardness of his proceedings; while, on the contrary, he assured him that there would be no hopes of it as long as they were not relieved of the fear of being made the victims of the oppression, and sacrificed to the envy of the Spanish nobles. At last Montigny's coadjutor made his appearance, and the objects of their embassy were made the subject of repeated deliberations.

1566. The king was at that time at his palace at Segovia, where also he assembled his state council. The members were: the Duke of Alva; Don Gomez de Figueroa; the Count of Feria; Don Antonio of Toledo, Grand Commander of St. John; Don John Manriquez of Lara, Lord Steward to the Queen; Ruy Gomez, Prince of Eboli and Count of Melito; Louis of Quixada, Master of the Horse to the Prince; Charles Tyssenacque, President of the Council for the Netherlands; Hopper, State Counsellor and Keeper of the Seal; and State Counsellor Corteville. The sitting of the council was protracted for several days; both ambassadors were in attendance, but the king was not himself present. Here, then, the conduct of the Belgian nobles was examined by Spanish eyes; step by step it was traced back to the most distant source; circumstances were brought into relation with others which, in reality, never had any connection; and what had been the offspring of the moment was made out to be a well-matured and far-sighted plan. All the different transactions and attempts of the nobles which had been governed solely by chance, and to which the natural order of events alone assigned their particular shape and succession, were said to be the result of a preconcerted scheme for introducing universal liberty in religion, and for placing all the power of the state in the hands of the nobles. The first step to this end was, it was said, the violent expulsion of the minister Granvella, against whom nothing could be charged, except that he was in possession of an authority which they preferred to exercise themselves. The second step was sending Count Egmont to Spain to urge the abolition of the Inquisition and the mitigation of the penal statutes, and to prevail on the king to consent to an augmentation of the council of state. As, however, this could not be surreptitiously obtained in so quiet a manner, the attempt was made to extort it from the court by a third and more daring step— by a formal conspiracy, the league of the Gueux. The fourth step to the same end was the present embassy, which at length boldly cast aside the mask, and by the insane proposals which they were not ashamed to make to their king, clearly brought to light the object to which all the preceding steps had tended. Could the abolition of the Inquisition, they exclaimed, lead to anything less than a complete freedom of belief? Would not the guiding helm of conscience be lost with it? Did not the proposed "moderation" introduce an absolute impunity for all heresies? What was the project of augmenting the council of state and of suppressing the two other councils but a complete remodelling of the government of the country in favor of the nobles? — a general constitution for all the provinces of the Netherlands? Again, what was this compact of the ecclesiastics in their public preachings but a third conspiracy, entered into with the very same objects which the league of the nobles in the council of state and that of the Gueux had failed to effect?

However, it was confessed that whatever might be the source of the evil it was not on that account the less important and imminent. The immediate personal presence of the king in Brussels was, indubitably, the most efficacious means speedily and thoroughly to remedy it. As, however, it was already so late in the year, and the preparations alone for the journey would occupy the short tine which was to elapse before the winter set in; as the stormy season of the year, as well as the danger from French and English ships, which rendered the sea unsafe, did not allow of the king's taking the northern route, which was the shorter of the two; as the rebels themselves meanwhile might become possessed of the island of Walcheren, and oppose the lauding of the king; for all these reasons, the journey was not to be thought of before the spring, and in absence of the only complete remedy it was necessary to rest satisfied with a partial expedient. The council, therefore, agreed to propose to the king, in the first place, that he should recall the papal Inquisition from the provinces and rest satisfied with that of the bishops; in the second place, that a new plan for the mitigation of the edicts should be projected, by which the honor of religion and of the king would be better preserved than it had been in the transmitted "moderation;" thirdly, that in order to reassure the minds of the people, and to leave no means untried, the king should impart to the regent full powers to extend free grace and pardon to all those who had not already committed any heinous crime, or who had not as yet been condemned by any judicial process; but from the benefit of this indemnity the preachers and all who harbored them were to be excepted. On the other hand, all leagues, associations, public assemblies, and preachings were to be henceforth prohibited under heavy penalties; if, however, this prohibition should be infringed, the regent was to be at liberty to employ the regular troops and garrisons for the forcible reduction of the refractory, and also, in case of necessity, to enlist new troops, and to name the commanders over them according as should be deemed advisable. Finally, it would have a good effect if his majesty would write to the most eminent towns, prelates, and leaders of the nobility, to some in his own hand, and to all in a gracious tone, in order to stimulate their zeal in his service.

When this resolution of his council of state was submitted to the king his first measure was to command public processions and prayers in all the most considerable places of the kingdom and also of the Netherlands, imploring the Divine guidance in his decision. He appeared in his own person in the council of state in order to approve this resolution and render it effective. He declared the general assembly of the states to be useless and entirely abolished it. He, however, bound himself to retain some German regiments in his pay, and, that they might serve with the more zeal, to pay them their long-standing arrears. He commanded the regent in a private letter to prepare secretly for war; three thousand horse and ten thousand infantry were to be assembled by her in Germany, to which end he furnished her with the necessary letters and transmitted to her a sum of three hundred thousand gold florins. He also accompanied this resolution with several autograph letters to some private individuals and towns, in which he thanked them in the most gracious terms for the zeal which they had already displayed in his service and called upon them to manifest the same for the future. Notwithstanding that he was inexorable on the most important point, and the very one on which the nation most particularly insisted — the convocation of the states, notwithstanding that his limited and ambiguous pardon was as good as none, and depended too much on arbitrary will to calm the public mind; notwithstanding, in fine, that he rejected, as too lenient, the proposed "moderation," but which, on the part of the people, was complained of as too severe; still he had this time made an unwonted step in the favor of the nation; he had sacrificed to it the papal Inquisition and left only the episcopal, to which it was accustomed. The nation had found more equitable judges in the Spanish council than they could reasonably have hoped for. Whether at another time and under other circumstances this wise concession would have had the desired effect we will not pretend to say. It came too late; when (1566) the royal letters reached Brussels the attack on images had already commenced.